UNDERSTANDING STRESS

UNDERSTANDING

STRESS

by Robert S. Feldman

A Venture Book
Franklin Watts
New York/London/Toronto/Sydney

Photographs copyright © : Randy Matusow: p. 13; Photo Researchers, Inc./
Barbara Rios: pp. 25, 81; Richard Hutchings/PhotoEdit: p. 28; AP/Wide World
Photos: p. 31; Comstock Photography, Inc./Sven Martson: p. 76.

Library of Congress Cataloging-in-Publication Data

Feldman, Robert S. (Robert Stephen), 1947–
Understanding stress / by Robert S. Feldman.
p.   cm. — (A Venture book)
Includes bibliographical references and index.
Summary: Describes the causes and effects of stress and ways of
preventing or dealing with it.
ISBN 0-531-12531-9
1. Stress (Psychology)—Juvenile literature.   2. Stress
(Psychology)—Prevention—Juvenile literature.   [1. Stress
(Psychology)]   I. Title.
BF575.S75F45   1992   91-38158
155.9′042—dc20   CIP   AC

CONTENTS

UNDERSTANDING STRESS

PART I

CAUSES OF

CHAPTER ONE

VICTIMS OF STRESS

Having to speak to a group of people was the worst thing Jerry Harmon could imagine. He didn't have any trouble talking with his friends, of course. But put Jerry in front of a group of classmates in school and he falls apart. His heart starts pounding, sweat drips from his forehead, and he can't remember a thing he was going to say.

Jerry was terrified at the thought of presenting a report to his class in two weeks. It didn't matter that he had plenty of time to prepare. He simply didn't want to do it. He felt like leaving town. He had never experienced such stress in his life.

For as long as she could remember, Helen MacDonald had enjoyed acting. When she landed one of the lead roles in her high school play, she was overjoyed.

Two weeks before the performance, though, Helen's feelings changed. She was nervous and frightened. She was having trouble remembering her lines. Her friends kept telling her how lucky she was to have a lead in the play, but that didn't help at all.

"How can this be?" she asked herself. "I wanted to be in this play more than anything. To get a lead is a dream come true. But now all I can think about is the stress I'm feeling."

Jerry's and Helen's situations are very different. One is an unpleasant, worrisome event; the other is the chance of a lifetime. Yet their reactions are the same: they both feel unbearable stress.

Stress is something we all live with. It keeps us awake at night. It makes us angry with others. It causes our hearts to pound and our stomachs to knot up. It also takes a long-term toll on our bodies and minds. In fact, experts think that many illnesses are related to stress. Every week, over 100 million people take drugs to relieve its symptoms. American industries lose $150 billion annually in stress-related costs.[1]

WHAT IS STRESS?

Most people would say they know what stress is. But for scientists who study stress, it has been surprisingly hard to define. This is because there are so many ways of looking at stress.

Some researchers have studied how our bodies react to stress. You know how your heart beats faster, you perspire more heavily, and your words don't come out right when you are placed in a stressful situation. But knowing how we feel when we experience stress does not explain it; nor does it tell us what causes it.

Other scientists have looked at *stressors:* events or situations that produce stress.[2] A deadline, a poor test performance, or bothersome noises all may be thought of as

You can see the tension in the faces of these young people backstage before a performance. Stress is often an integral part of life's challenges. When we deal successfully with such stress, we grow.

stressors. Even pleasant events can be stressors. Planning a party or starting a new job can be just as stressful as being called to the principal's office.

Stress, then, can be caused by both negative and positive events, or stressors. Of course, whether an event is thought of as positive or negative is in some ways a matter of personal choice. To people like Jerry Harmon, public speaking is an entirely unpleasant event. Other people, though, would be delighted to have a chance to have an audience to speak to. Unlike Jerry, those people would not consider public speaking stressful.

In sum, it is the way people interpret an event that makes it stressful or not stressful. This process of interpretation is called *appraisal*. Depending on how people appraise, or judge, circumstances, they may or may not consider them stressful.

What, specifically, causes people to appraise a situation as stressful? The answer depends on how much of a threat or a challenge it appears to be. Circumstances that pose a threat or challenge to a person's sense of well-being produce stress. Those that do not threaten or challenge us are not stressful.[3]

Looking at stress this way gives us a general definition of the concept of stress: *Stress is a response to circumstances that seem threatening or challenging.*

The circumstances that cause stress vary from one person to another. It all depends on how we appraise circumstances. In addition, the things that cause us stress today may not cause us stress at another time. And the opposite is true: things that once caused no stress may now be stressful.

Consider a young boy who enjoys playing with dogs. Suppose he was playing in his backyard one day and a stray dog ran up and bit him. That experience would change his feelings about dogs. Instead of bringing him joy as it once did, the sight of a dog would produce stress.

WHAT PRODUCES STRESS?

How do we know which situations produce stress and which do not? There are several things that stressors share.[4]

Situations we cannot control are more likely to produce stress than situations we can control. When we are talking about stress, "control" means that we are able to change what happens in a situation. When we do not have control, we feel we are at the mercy of events or other people. This can produce a great deal of stress.

For example, think about these two teachers who are very demanding of their students: Mrs. McPhee is open to reason and can be argued with, and she sometimes changes her mind after listening to what students have to say. Mr. Monroe, on the other hand, does not pay attention to students' ideas, and he never changes his mind about what he wants the students to do. His students have little control over the situation.

Mr. Monroe's class is obviously more stressful for students. Mrs. McPhee's students, in contrast, feel that they have a say in what takes place. They are more relaxed in class.

Unpredictable circumstances produce greater stress than circumstances that are predictable. Suppose you had a job in which you could never tell how the boss was going to react. On some days, he might come into the office and be angry with everyone and the smallest problem might anger him. On the other hand, on some days he might be nice and friendly. But you could never tell in advance what his mood would be. Such a situation would clearly be stressful.

Even negative events are less stressful if they are predictable. Scientists studying stress have carried out experiments that expose people to bursts of loud noise. They have found that the greatest stress occurs when the bursts are unpredictable. As long as people can predict in advance when the noise is going to occur, they are able to adjust to it.

Circumstances that are unclear and vague produce more stress than circumstances that are clear-cut. Suppose you were asked to plan a large birthday party for your six-year-old sister, but you were given no further instructions or ideas. You would be under much more stress than if you had a list of things to include or some useful ideas about what was expected. If demands are not clear, we experience stress.

Stress adds up over time. A weak source of stress may grow into a powerful stressor over time. In fact, repeated exposure to a weak stressor may produce more stress than exposure to a powerful one-time stressor.

When we know that stress is due to a temporary situation, we are better able to adjust to it. On the other hand, when the source of stress seems endless, our ability to cope with it is not as good.

Unscheduled events produce greater stress than scheduled events. Unscheduled events occur without warning; they come by surprise. For example, the accidental injury or death of a loved one comes unexpectedly. Such events produce great stress, since we cannot prepare for them.

On the other hand, we can ready ourselves for events that are scheduled in advance. You know that someday you will graduate from school and get a job. When that time comes, you probably will be ready. Preparation reduces stress.

The circumstances that are most likely to produce stress are negative ones. Positive events can produce stress, but negative ones are generally more stressful. In part, negative events are more likely to cause stress because they place more demands on us. We actively try to avoid negative events. When they occur, we have to find a way to solve the problem. This takes time, effort, and energy. In sum, it is stressful.

On the other hand, we are eager to face the challenge of positive events (a summer away from home, a solo in a concert). In most cases, we look forward to them. Facing the challenge may be stressful, but it is a pleasant task.

HOW STRESS AFFECTS US

As we will see in detail later in this book, stress affects us in many ways. It can be harmful to both physical and mental health.

Physically, stress makes the body work less efficiently. In the worst cases, too much stress can bring about serious illness and even death.

Psychologists, experts who focus on mental health, consider how stress affects our behavior and emotions. They look at how stressors produce *anxiety,* an emotion in which we feel fear and worry. Stress causes us to be upset and feel frightened. Too much stress can make us unable to think clearly and lead normal lives.

In sum, stress produces declines in both physical and mental health. Part of the challenge in understanding stress is that its effects are so powerful and broad.

In future chapters, we will discuss ways of understanding and coping with stress. We begin by looking at the causes of stress. We will see that many types of situations produce stress.

Next, we will discuss the effects of stress. We will see how our bodies and minds react to stress and how stress can cause disease and illness.

Finally, we will consider ways of coping with stress. All of us can benefit from a reduction of stress in our lives, and we will discover that there are many ways to keep stress to a minimum.

CHAPTER TWO

EVERYDAY STRESS

6:30 A.M. Alarm rings. Fight with younger brother for bathroom. Grab breakfast and run down street to catch school bus.

7:20 A.M. Homeroom. Finish homework assignment for German class, first period.

9:25 A.M. Take biology test.

11:25 A.M. Eat lunch: tuna sandwich and two Twinkies.

1:30 P.M. Math teacher says she'll hand back last week's test at end of period. After waiting forty-five minutes, get test back and find it graded a C −.

2:30 P.M. Work on school newspaper, with a printer's deadline to meet at 4:30 P.M.

4:30 P.M. Catch bus home and start homework.

6:10 P.M. Eat dinner. Tell parents about C − on test, facing their anger.

7:00 P.M. Continue homework, hoping to be interrupted by invitation to a party the next weekend. No phone calls.

9:00 P.M. Watch an hour of television.

10:00 P.M. Bedtime. Suddenly remember tomorrow's science quiz and stay up another half hour studying.

Does this sound like your life? If it does—as it does for many students—you probably experience a good deal of stress.

While we usually think that it is unusual, out-of-the-ordinary events that produce stress, in fact everyday activities may produce as much, or even more, stress than one-time events. Even such routine, everyday activities as catching a school bus may be a source of stress.

To understand the different sources of stress people experience, we need to distinguish between two major types of stressors: personal stressors and background stressors.[1] *Personal stressors* are major events in a person's life. The death of a parent, a major school failure, or the abrupt end of a deep personal relationship are examples of personal stressors.

In contrast, *background stressors,* which are sometimes called *daily hassles,* are minor irritations of life that we all face from time to time. Being stuck in a long cafeteria line or having a pencil break in the middle of a test are examples of background stressors. Because the results of exposure to personal stressors and background stressors are different, we need to consider the two separately.

LIFE'S MAJOR CHALLENGES: PERSONAL STRESSORS

What are the most stressful things that could happen to you? Although each of us may come up with slightly different lists of personal stressors, there would likely be many similarities. Two physicians, Thomas Holmes and Richard Rahe, were the first to attempt to develop a list of common life events—both negative and positive—that are the most typical sources of stress in adults.[2] Later research has extended their initial findings, and stress experts have developed lists which indicate the most stressful events in the lives of adolescents, such as the one shown in Table 2-1. All the events have something in common: each represents a change in the circumstances of life.

Of course, not all life events represent the same amount of change. Nor do they bring about the same degree of stress. For instance, being told that you are attractive to a friend is clearly not in the same league as the death of a parent. Because some stressors have more of an impact than others, each of the personal stressors has a numerical value attached to it.

The numbers in the table are called Life Change Units (LCUs) and they range from 108 (the death of a parent) to 18 (being invited to join a social organization). It is also noteworthy that the list includes both negative events and positive ones. As we discussed in Chapter 1, stress can be brought about by both negative and positive circumstances.

Assigning LCUs allows us to add up each of the stressors in a person's life and get an idea of that individual's personal stress level. For example, suppose you are invited to join a social organization (18 LCUs) and soon afterward go on the first date of your life (42 LCUs). The total stress you experience would be 60 LCUs. In addition, because all LCUs are supposed to be similar, your total stress level is roughly equivalent to that brought about by the death of a close friend (63 LCUs) during the same period of time.

By knowing the total number of LCUs experienced in a given period of time, researchers have been able to study how that stress is related to other factors. They have found some consistent results.

Most important, it appears that the total number of LCUs is related to declining health.[3] The more LCUs, the greater the likelihood of major physical illness.

Table 2-1
Sources of Stress *

This is a list of the most important and common sources of stress in the lives of adolescents and a number showing how stressful each one is. Remember that these are only estimates.

Life Change Units
   (LCUs)

LCUs	Source
108	The death of a parent
88	The death of a brother or sister
88	Getting pregnant
78	Getting married
70	Divorce of your parents
63	Death of a close friend
62	Marital separation of your parents
61	Fathering a pregnancy
52	The death of a grandparent
52	Hospitalization of a parent
51	Remarriage of a parent to a stepparent
50	Birth of a brother or sister
50	Being hospitalized for illness or injury
49	Hospitalization of a brother or sister
47	Failing a grade in school
46	Loss of a job by your father or mother
46	Being sent away from home
45	Becoming involved with drugs
43	Start of a new problem between you and your parents
42	Going on the first date of your life
41	Start of a new problem between your parents
41	Move to a new school district
41	Major increase in your parents' income
41	Major decrease in your parents' income

Table 2-1 (*Continued*)

Life Change Units
(LCUs)

LCUs	
41	Deciding to leave home
40	Getting your first permanent job
39	Outstanding personal achievement (special prize)
39	Breaking up with a boy/girlfriend
39	Being accepted at the college of your choice
36	Being responsible for an automobile accident
35	End of a problem between you and your parents
35	Getting a summer job
35	Change in father's job so he has less time home
35	Being told to break up with a boy/girl-friend
34	Suspension from school
34	Finding a new dating partner
34	A new adult moving into your home
33	Graduating from high school
32	Getting your first driver's license
32	Failing to achieve something you really wanted
31	Appearance in a juvenile court
30	Stopping the use of drugs
30	End of a problem between your parents
28	Mother beginning to work outside the home
26	Being told you are very attractive by a friend

Life Change Units
    (LCUs)

25	Becoming an adult member of a church
24	Recognition for excelling in a sport or other activity
22	Finding an adult who really respects you
21	Being invited by a friend to break the law
19	Beginning the first year of senior high school
18	Being invited to join a social organization

*From R. D. Coddington, "Measuring the Stressfulness of a Child's Environment," in J. H. Humphrey, ed., *Stress in Childhood* (New York: AMS Press, 1984).

Before you start to add up your own LCUs, you should be aware that some researchers have doubts about just how accurate the Life Change Unit values are.[4] Is it reasonable to assume that the death of a friend is just a little more stressful than the combination of being asked to join a social organization and having a first date? Is it realistic to suggest that experiencing an increase in your parents' income is really more stressful than having to appear in juvenile court? You can see that the scale may be useful only to a limited extent.

Stress is an individual matter. Each of us evaluates events in his own way. We even change the way we react to certain situations over the course of our lives. Many a politician who gives stirring speeches to large crowds found public speaking agonizingly stressful at a younger age.

In sum, it is important to keep in mind that the specific numbers given to events in the Life Change Unit scale may differ from one person to another. Even more important, we need to be aware that some people's stressors may not even be included on the scale. For example, some people may find a decrease in time spent alone to be stressful. The Life Change Unit scale includes no score for such a change.

In spite of these drawbacks, the Life Change Unit scale does provide a fairly complete list of life's major personal stressors. But remember that these account for only the stressors related to major events in our lives.

What of the lingering, everyday kinds of annoyances that we all face? Isn't it possible that they may add up and eventually produce as much stress as the personal stressors listed on the Life Change Unit scale? To answer these questions, we need to consider what we have called "background stressors" or, more informally, "daily hassles."

LIFE'S DAILY HASSLES: BACKGROUND STRESSORS

"I gained three pounds again, and
I've got to take them off."

"My mom nags me all the time."

"I've got too much to do. I'll never
finish my book report on time."

If any of these things sounds familiar, you're well acquainted with background stressors. As we pointed out earlier, these daily hassles are the minor irritations of life. When you are delayed by a long line at the supermarket, or the trash collectors wake you up by banging the garbage cans, or your younger brother teases you one more time about your hair, you are being exposed to a daily hassle.

**An example of a daily hassle: waiting on line
and checking out at the supermarket**

Other daily hassles may be long-term, recurring problems. Dissatisfaction with school or teachers, an unhappy boyfriend-girlfriend relationship, or having to share a room with a sibling can be thought of as daily hassles.

By itself, each daily hassle does not produce all that much stress. It is when it occurs along with other daily hassles that the stress adds up—and in a big way. In fact, daily hassles may take as great a toll on a person's psychological and physical well-being as would a single major personal stressor.

Daily hassles produce a variety of outcomes. The more daily hassles a person faces, the more unpleasant emotions and moods he or she experiences.[5] In addition, health problems such as flu, sore throats, headaches, and backaches have been linked to the number of daily hassles in a person's life.

What are the most frequent daily hassles for adults? Surveys show that several problems crop up over and over. As you can see in Table 2-2, concerns about weight and health, along with economic doubts, top the list.

As with personal stressors, it is important to keep in mind that the nature of daily hassles differs from one person to another. To a thin person who has never had a weight problem, gaining a few pounds may be a cause for curiosity rather than concern. Like major stressors, the things that are daily hassles at one point in a person's life may not be problems later. What we perceive as daily hassles, then, shifts during the course of our lives.

Probably the major factor that determines whether an unpleasant situation is seen as a daily hassle is how much control we have over it. Disagreeable situations that we have little or no control over are likely to be viewed as more troublesome than situations we can control.

Suppose you lived in a house near a small airport and airplanes flew over night and day at seemingly random intervals. You might reasonably view the flights as a constant daily hassle. But imagine you joined a neighborhood

Table 2-2
The Ten Most Frequent Daily Hassles*

1. Concerns about weight
2. Health of a family member
3. Rising price of common goods
4. Home maintenance
5. Too many things to do
6. Misplacing or losing things
7. Yard work or major outside home maintenance
8. Property investment or taxes
9. Fears of crime
10. Physical appearance

*From A. D. Kanner, J. C. Coyne, C. Schaefer, and R. S. Lazarus, "Comparison of Two Modes of Stress Measurement: Daily Hassles and Uplifts versus Major Life Events," *Journal of Behavioral Medicine* 4 (1981), p. 14, Table 3. Reprinted with permission.

organization that was successful in restricting the flights to just certain hours of the day and banning them entirely at night. It is likely that you would then judge the airplane noise as less of a hassle. In fact, even if there were as many airplane takeoffs and landings as before and the total amount of noise didn't change, it is likely that you would experience less overall stress.

Your stress level would decrease because you had gained control over the pattern of flights. Even though the total amount of noise was the same, you would now feel that to a certain extent *you* were in charge.

THE HIGHS OF LIFE: UPLIFTS

If life were made up of nothing but daily hassles, it would not be much fun. Happily, though, we experience a variety of minor events that make us feel good. These are called *uplifts*.

Uplifts range from such things as seeing a beautiful

A laugh shared with friends over lunch is an
example of one of the little uplifts that help
to counteract the hassles of a typical day.

Table 2-3
The Ten Most Frequent Uplifts*

1. Relating well with spouse or lover
2. Relating well with friends
3. Completing a task
4. Feeling healthy
5. Getting enough sleep
6. Eating out
7. Meeting your responsibilities
8. Visiting, phoning, or writing someone
9. Spending time with family
10. Home (inside) pleasing to you

*From A. D. Kanner, J. C. Coyne, C. Schaefer, and R. S. Lazarus, "Comparison of Two Modes of Stress Measurement: Daily Hassles and Uplifts versus Major Life Events," *Journal of Behavioral Medicine* 4 (1981), p. 14, Table 3. Reprinted with permission.

view to receiving a sincere compliment. As you can see from the list of the most frequent uplifts revealed by surveys of adults (Table 2-3), uplifts do not represent major events in people's lives. However, they do make a difference.

In fact, uplifts seem to serve as protection against the hassles of life. They are associated with good health. The more uplifts people experience, the better their psychological and physical health.

As is the case with hassles, uplifts are personal. What is an uplift for one person may be another person's hassle.

The most important thing about uplifts is that they may help us reduce the harmful outcomes of stress in other areas. Since no one's life is entirely free of stress, these stress reducers are useful to all of us.

CHAPTER THREE

EXTREME STRESS: CATASTROPHES AND NATURAL DISASTERS

For most San Franciscans, October 17, 1989, was a routine day. Routine, that is, until 5:04 P.M., when the ground literally began to shake under their feet. It wasn't the "big one," a quake the size of the 1906 earthquake that geologists say will probably strike the city within the next thirty years. But it was bad enough to cause huge amounts of property damage—and to produce devastating, lingering stress for millions of people.

Many catastrophes and natural disasters last only a few seconds but their effects on survivors often last a lifetime. Even after the immediate danger has passed, survivors of disasters may suffer long-term consequences. They may experience serious emotional difficulties, health problems, and other symptoms of stress.

In the last chapter we discussed the two kinds of stressors—personal stressors and background stressors—that we all experience. Most people are lucky enough never to experience a major catastrophe. When they do and survive, the effects of the stress may be severe.

A San Francisco woman searches through the wreckage of her apartment after the devastating 1989 earthquake. The stress that victims of natural and technological disasters incur can linger for years.

DISASTERS: NATURAL AND MAN-MADE

Some catastrophes are caused by natural disasters, while others are caused by technological failures. How much stress we feel following a catastrophe depends on which kind of disaster it was. Natural disasters, such as hurricanes and tornadoes, produce less stress than technological disasters, such as the explosion of a nuclear reactor or a breakdown of a dam due to faulty design.[1]

In one example of this, a group of researchers interviewed people who were exposed to chemicals leaking from a toxic-waste dump. They compared their reactions to those of people in a nearby community who were victims of a flood.

A year after their respective disasters, the victims of the chemical-waste leak were still experiencing a high amount of stress, while the flood survivors showed significantly less stress.

There are several reasons that natural disasters produce less stress than technological disasters.[2] Natural disasters are seen as largely unpreventable. We cannot avoid a tornado, and we cannot blame it on anyone else. Natural disasters are totally chance events that we are unable to escape. However, we usually think that technological disasters could have been prevented. When an explosion occurs in a nuclear reactor, we can blame the engineers who designed it or the technicians who did not pay enough attention to a breakdown. Victims of such disasters are angry, and they blame those they think could have prevented them.

There is another reason natural disasters produce less stress than technological disasters. Natural disasters usually have a clear beginning and ending. For example, when a hurricane comes, it gradually gets stronger and stronger, but finally it fades and the sun comes out.

Technological disasters, on the other hand, often have no clear start or finish. If you were exposed to a chemical waste dump, for instance, you might not know when the danger began. In addition, you might wonder for the rest of your life whether you were poisoned by the exposure. Your inability to pinpoint the beginning and end of the disaster would produce high levels of stress that would continue indefinitely.

Probably the most important reason that technological disasters produce greater stress than natural disasters has to do with our sense of control over the world. You'll remember how we talked in earlier chapters about the importance of control over what happens to us. We discussed that the greater the sense of control we have, the lower the stress we experience.

Now think about what happens when a technological disaster occurs. Because we usually think that we—or at least other people—should have control over the technological innovations that are designed to improve our lives, we experience a particularly strong sense of loss of control when such technology breaks down. On the other hand, when a natural disaster occurs, we experience less of a loss of control because we never felt a strong sense of control over them in the first place.

THE STAGES OF STRESS FOLLOWING A CATASTROPHE

No matter what kind of catastrophe or natural disaster we undergo, the stress we experience afterward usually follows a set pattern, or series of stages.[3] The first and most rapid reaction is that of *outcry,* in which victims feel fear, sadness, or rage. They usually feel that they have been singled out wrongfully, and that they are undeserving of what has happened to them. Life seems unfair to them.

Following this instant reaction, though, victims enter a curious stage of *denial.* Feeling dazed and shocked by the experience, they try to forget what has happened by refusing to face their memories of the disaster. Important facts and details about the event may be forgotten. Victims may even deny to themselves that they or others were hurt by the disaster—even though their injuries may be quite obvious.

In some cases, denial is shown by a general lessening of all emotions. In others, denial takes the form of an inability to concentrate or a refusal to talk about subjects that are even slightly related to the disaster.

In the normal course of events, denial is replaced by the next stage, *intrusive thoughts,* in which memories of the disaster interfere with everyday living. Victims cannot forget particular images of the event. These thoughts interfere with situations that are unrelated to the disaster. In some ways, the intrusive-thoughts stage is the opposite of the denial stage.

Interestingly, people often move back and forth between the stages of denial and intrusive thoughts. Some days they do not think at all about the disaster, denying to themselves it ever happened. Other days, though, they can think of nothing but the disaster.

Eventually, most survivors of a catastrophe move into a *coping* stage, in which they are able to face the reality of what happened. They come to grips with the consequences of the disaster. Some individuals even grow from the experience, learning things that help them lead better lives.

Unfortunately, though, not everyone is able to deal successfully with the consequences of a disaster. Some people get ''stuck'' at one of the early stages of the stress process. For instance, some victims continually refuse to think about the disaster. They may not even try to get help that is easily available to them, such as applying for funds to repair a house damaged by a flood. Or they may be unable to experience either positive or negative emotions because they are trying so hard to hide their emotional reactions from themselves.

Other people may think of nothing but the disaster,

wanting to discuss the event over and over, even months later. They may continually relive the disaster. This constant emotion may be overwhelming and may disrupt their lives, preventing them from recovering.

For some people, then, living through a major disaster produces long-term difficulties. These complications may result in lasting physical or mental health problems—or both.

DISASTERS AND PHYSICAL HEALTH

The stress caused by a disaster produces declines in many victims' physical health. Certain problems, of course, occur immediately. For example, some individuals sustain injuries during the catastrophe itself or in its immediate aftermath. Other people suffer from secondary illnesses that are a result of disruption of food and water supplies brought about by the disaster.

In some cases, health problems don't seem related to the disaster. For instance, some victims have a vitamin deficiency long after a catastrophe has occurred. Studies of people living close to the Three Mile Island nuclear power plant, which malfunctioned in 1979, discovered that residents showed some subtle changes in the chemical makeup of their bodies.[4] The researchers found that people living close to the damaged plant showed higher than normal levels of a chemical called catecholamine. Catecholamine is released as a result of stress.

Sometimes, the physical consequences of being in a disaster are very obvious. One study of survivors of a flood in England found that in the year following the flood, victims were more likely to require surgery and to suffer from poorer overall health than nonvictims. The death rate was also higher for people who had lived through the flood than for people who lived in the same area but had not been directly affected by it.[5]

When victims of disasters are asked to describe the

state of their physical health, they usually respond that they are less healthy than they were before the disaster occurred. They also feel they are less healthy than those who have not undergone a disaster.

DISASTERS AND MENTAL HEALTH

While some victims of disasters experience primarily physical problems, some have long-lasting mental health difficulties. Among the most common reactions—which occur in up to one third of all victims—are feelings of grief, anxiety, anger, hostility, or depression. Some people show little emotion, or they become inactive. Others demonstrate a lack of ambition and drive.

Other people react to disaster by turning to alcohol, tranquilizers, or illegal drugs, or by quarreling with family members. Victims may have trouble sleeping. Children may be especially affected: they may be unable to get to sleep or have nightmares or they may lose interest in school.

Adolescent victims sometimes avoid dating and have trouble concentrating in school. Some act irresponsibly, while others show reckless and even illegal behavior. Some imagine they have physical problems, complaining of one illness after another when nothing is really wrong.

One aftermath of especially severe disasters is "survivor guilt." Survivors of disasters may feel guilty that they were spared while others were killed. They feel guilty because they think of themselves as no more deserving to live than those who died.

POSTTRAUMATIC STRESS DISORDER

A man fired from his job with an air cargo company returned to his office the following day dressed in an army uniform and carrying a shotgun. For close to two hours he held his former boss hostage and fired shots wildly. When captured, he said that he had just seen the movie *Platoon,* which brought back terrifying memories of Vietnam. His claim: He was suffering from an ailment called posttraumatic stress disorder, in which he was victimized by stress from wartime experiences.[6]

Posttraumatic stress disorder occurs when victims of major disasters "reexperience" the original stress event later. They may feel the emotions they experienced during the event, and they may see visual images and hear sounds that occurred.

Almost anything can trigger an episode of posttraumatic stress disorder. A noise, an image, or even a certain smell can lead a victim to recall the original disaster in vivid detail. In some cases, people dream about the disaster and wake up sweating and screaming. The dreams are so frightening that some people are afraid to go to sleep.

In other cases, people may feel extremely anxious but not know why. It is only much later that the reason for their anxiety, a past disaster, becomes clear to them.

Although posttraumatic stress disorder can occur after any disaster, it is most often seen in people who have had disastrous wartime experiences. Veterans of the Vietnam War are especially likely to have symptoms of the disorder.[7] This may explain why the suicide rate for Vietnam veterans is almost twice as high as it is for nonveterans. Posttraumatic stress syndrome has been blamed for many violent acts.

PART II

THE CONSEQUENCES OF STRESS

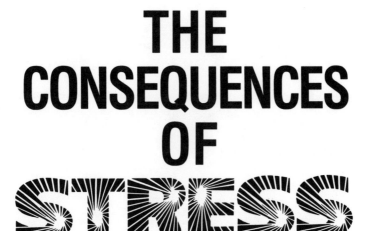

CHAPTER FOUR

REACTING TO STRESS

As Maria Torres struggled to finish her report for the next day's class, she rushed one last time to the library, just before it was due to close for the day. It would be a close call, but she thought she could finish on time—as long as she could look at the encyclopedia one more time.

Maria entered the library feeling exhausted. Her exhaustion soon turned to horror, though, when she looked at the rack of encyclopedias. The volume she needed was missing and nowhere in sight. Suddenly wide awake, she quickly began searching for the librarian, who was already beginning to lock up.

Although she might not have shown it, Maria was probably churning inside. But her reactions were not to fear alone; her body was helping to prepare her to deal with the sudden crisis.

To understand just what Maria's physical reactions were, we need to consider some basic human biology. One major part of the brain controls the functions of the body automatically. It makes our hearts pump blood and our lungs inhale and exhale constantly. We need not worry about these functions, because they occur mechanically.

The part of the body that controls these automatic functions is divided into two parts. The first part is called the *sympathetic division*. One of the major activities of the sympathetic division is to prepare the body to respond to emergency situations.

For example, suppose you were walking down a dark street and saw a stranger carrying what looked like a knife in the moonlight. As you experienced fear and tried to evaluate the situation, your sympathetic division would shift into high gear. Your heart rate would increase. You would begin to sweat. Your rate of breathing would increase. You would feel goose bumps all over your body.

The increase in activity of the sympathetic division is to prepare you to deal with the emergency. Your body is readying itself to fight off the stranger or to flee the situation. This is called the *fight-or-flight* response.[1] In either alternative, the sympathetic division makes sure that the body is at peak form to deal with the situation.

Once the emergency is over, it is the *parasympathetic division* of the brain that brings the body functions back to their normal levels. The parasympathetic division calms the body, returning it to normal after the emergency has ended.

Stress is closely tied to the sympathetic and parasympathetic divisions. This is because the first response to stress is similar to the body's response in an emergency situation.

When we experience stress, all the physical reactions that occur in an emergency happen. We could expect, then, that Maria Torres's response to the stress was to trigger her sympathetic division.

At first, the activation of the sympathetic division is

a helpful reaction. In fact, it may allow us to deal with the stressor effectively. In Maria's case, it might give her the energy to deal quickly with the situation.

Over time, though, long-term exposure to a stressor can be harmful. In fact, it can lay the groundwork for future health problems. When the sympathetic division is activated too much, it causes wear and tear on the body. For example, if a person's heart rate is frequently increased because of a sympathetic division reaction to stress, the heart can be weakened. Repeated stressors, then, may produce health problems.

THE GENERAL ADAPTATION SYNDROME

Hans Selye (pronounced sell-yea) was a pioneer in the field of stress. He developed a theory that has been very useful in explaining the effects of stress, no matter what the cause.

Selye's theory is called the *General Adaptation Syndrome (GAS).*[2] The core of the theory is an assumption that the same physical reactions to stress occur no matter how different the sources of the stress are.

Look, for a moment, at the diagram of the GAS in Figure 4-1. You can see that there are three stages in people's reactions to stress.

ALARM AND MOBILIZATION

The first stage of the model, *alarm and mobilization,* begins when people become aware of a threat or stressor, such as receiving a bad grade on a test, hearing their parents discussing divorce, or even experiencing something pleasant but challenging, such as an invitation to be an usher or a bridesmaid in a cousin's wedding.

The GAS model suggests that regardless of the kind of stress encountered, the body reacts in a similar way, energizing the pituitary gland and adrenal cortex hormonal system. The activation of the pituitary-adrenal cortex sys-

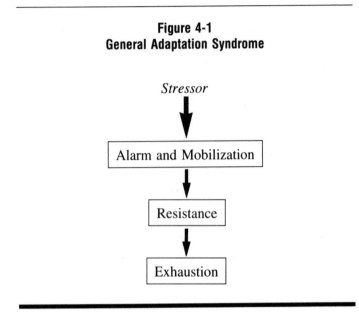

Figure 4-1
General Adaptation Syndrome

Stressor

Alarm and Mobilization

Resistance

Exhaustion

tem may lead to such symptoms as sores in the stomach or problems of the blood circulation system, and the body becomes vulnerable to a host of diseases.

However, if the stress does not overwhelm them, people can begin to mobilize their defenses against the stressor, making an effort to deal with the threat. For example, if you have received a poor grade, you might make plans to study harder in the future. This allows you to move into the next stage: resistance.

RESISTANCE

In the second stage, *resistance,* the body actively attempts to fight off or deal with the stressor. During this stage, the body reverses course from its initial reaction to the stressor. For example, during the alarm stage, the cells of the adrenal cortex release certain chemicals into the blood that leave the cortex deprived of that chemical. During the resistance stage, however, it increases its store of the same chemicals that it released during the alarm stage.

The goal during the resistance stage is to meet the challenge raised by the stressor. If people are successful in this stage, they may learn to adapt to the stressor, and it becomes less threatening. For instance, to improve a poor grade that you receive, you might decide to spend more time studying.

In some cases, however, people are not successful in their efforts to deal with stressors and the situation continues to strain their physical and psychological resources. When this happens, the third stage is reached.

EXHAUSTION

The third stage of Selye's theory, *exhaustion*, occurs when people face long-term stressors—and are unable to deal with them successfully.

In this stage, people more or less "wear out." They lose the physical energy to fight the stressor, and resistance is no longer possible. Usually, this results in physical illness.

Let's say you worked out a detailed study schedule for the future. Such behavior would be a clear sign of resistance. But suppose you continued to receive poor grades. Your next step might be to put even more effort and energy into studying. If you still were not successful, though, your ability to resist would eventually decline. Your long hours of studying would begin to take their toll, and your energy resources would be exhausted. Under these conditions, it is easy to imagine how you might become ill.

It is important to keep in mind that our response to stressors does not always reach the third stage. If we successfully resist the stressor's challenge during the second stage, our physical resources are not drained and we can bounce back. It is only when we can't cope with the stressor that we move into the exhaustion stage.

How do we get beyond the exhaustion stage? In many cases, being exhausted means that we are excused from having to meet a stressor head-on. For instance, people who study so hard that they become ill may be excused temporarily from completing their school assignments. At least for a while, then, the immediate stress is reduced.

In the long run, though, exhaustion is only a temporary cure for stress. After people recover from this stage, they must again face the stressor—or even new ones.

In summary, Hans Selye's General Adaptation Syndrome theory of stress says that people's reactions to stress proceed in three stages. The first, alarm and mobilization, consists of reacting physically to the stressor but then activating the body's efforts to deal with the stressor. The second stage, resistance, energizes people to cope with the challenge of the stressor. Finally, if they are not successful in dealing with the stressor, they move into the exhaustion stage, using up their physical resources. They are no longer able to show any resistance to the stressor.

It is important to remember that Selye's description of the GAS is still theory, not fact. It has not been proven. In fact, some experts on stress have criticized parts of his theory.[3]

One of the main objections to the GAS concerns the first stage, alarm and mobilization. The theory states that all stressors produce the same kind of physical reaction, no matter what kind of stressor is present. Is this accurate?

Some experts say no. They point to experimental evidence that certain stressors produce one sort of physical reaction while other stressors produce other kinds.

If these experts are correct, the GAS needs to be revised. However, it is too early to tell which point of view is right. Experiments have not been precise enough to answer the question once and for all.

The other major criticism of the GAS is that it seems to some experts to be incomplete. The GAS emphasizes people's physical reactions to stress, but says little about their psychological responses.

Many stress researchers think that our psychological reactions to stressors are at least as important as our physical ones. For these experts, the best way to understand how we respond to stress is to look at the mind and not the body. As we have seen, the way we perceive and interpret an event determines whether we find it stressful. Perception and interpretation are psychological factors, not physical factors.

In spite of the criticisms that have been made of the GAS, it is still our most important theory of stress. It provides a link between stressors on one hand and physical reactions on the other.

CHAPTER FIVE

STRESS AND ILLNESS

At the age of eighteen, Harry Bosworth was not a popular person. He was unhappy, and he had few friends. One day, Harry's problems got far worse: he was hit in the eye during a snowball fight. The snowball left him blind, and he was unable to study. The injury caused him to leave school.

Over time, his eyesight improved and he tried to find work. However, he found that his eyesight worsened each time he looked for a job. Strangely, though, soon after he gave up his job search, his eyesight returned.

This pattern continued for four years. Whenever he looked for work, he became blind; but as long as he didn't try to find a job or to study, his eyesight was normal.[1]

If Harry's blindness strikes you as puzzling, you are not alone. His physicians were also mystified. They found nothing wrong with his eyes.

Harry's doctors eventually concluded that he suffered from a *psychosomatic* (sy-ko-so-Ma-tik) disorder, a physical disorder in which emotions and thoughts play an important role.

Harry's specific problem is known as *conversion disorder*. In a conversion disorder, patients convert an emotional problem into a physical one; there is no physical cause for the medical problem.

The conversion disorder starts when people feel stress and anxiety that they aren't able to cope with. The physical problem that results often gives them an excuse to avoid the stressor that produces the anxiety.

For example, Harry Bosworth's blindness conveniently allowed him to avoid situations that were quite stressful. He could no longer attend school, and he could not get a job. Even though his unemployment may eventually have become stressful itself, having no job was probably less stressful than attending school or working.

Sometimes people get conversion disorders in groups. In one case, a group of student pilots in the U.S. Navy developed problems with their eyesight.[2] Their vision became blurry, and they had trouble focusing.

Doctors could find nothing wrong to cause their vision problems. It turned out to be a group case of conversion disorder. The student pilots were under a lot of stress, but they felt that quitting the program to avoid the stress was too embarrassing. Instead, they developed physical symptoms that allowed them to leave the program without embarrassment.

Do people with conversion disorders know they are translating problems caused by stress and anxiety into physical ailments? The answer is no. They do not realize the true cause of their physical problems and believe they are actually sick.

One way we know that a conversion disorder has occurred is by looking at people's reactions to their symptoms. People with conversion disorders react to their medical problems in an unusual way: they seem to be not bothered much by them. For instance, a person who wakes up deaf one morning might not seem to care much about it. Clearly, such a reaction is odd. Think how you might feel if you woke one morning and were no longer able to hear!

In sum, conversion disorders occur when people translate emotional problems into physical illness. However, when physicians take a close look at patients who have conversion disorders, they are unable to find any problem or damage to the body that might account for the symptoms. The symptoms of conversion disorders are produced by stress, then, but there is no actual physical damage to the body.

In many cases, however, stress actually does cause real physical damage to the body. We turn now to some specific diseases that are produced or affected by stress.

STRESS-RELATED ILLNESS

STOMACH PROBLEMS AND ULCERS

You may have heard younger brothers or sisters complaining of stomachaches whenever they did not want to go to school. Although you might have thought they were faking, in fact their symptoms could have been quite real.

Some of the most frequent physical problems related to stress are centered on stomach distress. For example, vomiting and diarrhea are frequent symptoms of stress in children.

In adults, one of the most common, and serious, stomach problems is ulcers. Ulcers are sores in the digestive tract that are constantly irritated when the stomach overproduces the digestive acid. The lining of the stomach breaks down in places, allowing sores to develop.

Because certain kinds of emotions are related to the development of ulcers, the illness is considered to be stress-related. Specifically, frequent worry, anger, and anxiety may cause ulcers. In addition, people who have ulcers often report that they are very busy or rushed and under stress.

Yet stress alone does not give us a full explanation for the development of ulcers. Not everyone who has high stress develops ulcers, and not everyone who develops ulcers has high levels of stress in their lives. Diet and family history also are related to the development of ulcers.

ARTHRITIS

Arthritis is a disease in which the joints of the body become swollen and inflamed. The hands, arms, and feet become painful and difficult to move. Some kinds of arthritis are made worse by stress. For example, depression and anxiety are related to increases in symptoms. An increase in the number of stressors in patients' lives may also lead to increases in the severity of arthritis.

HEADACHES

Among the most universal medical problems are headaches. Most headaches are related to emotional tension and anxiety, having no clear medical cause.[3]

There are actually several kinds of headaches. The most painful are migraine headaches. During a migraine, there is a reduced flow of blood to the brain as blood vessels constrict. This is followed by a sudden surge of blood into the brain, causing a rapid expansion of the blood vessels—and often severe pain.

Other headaches are known as tension headaches, caused when muscles in the scalp contract. In turn, the blood vessels of the brain are compressed, causing pain.

Migraine and tension headaches usually occur for the first time during the teenage years. They also happen most frequently during times of unusual stress. In fact, headaches are thought to be one of the most frequent indicators of stress and tension in people's lives.

HIGH BLOOD PRESSURE

High blood pressure is a disease in which the force of the blood surging through the body's blood vessels becomes too great. This places strain on the walls of the blood vessels and can cause them and the heart to weaken.

We all experience temporary increases in blood pressure, since it is part of the emergency reaction that accompanies stressful situations. In some people, though, blood pressure stays habitually high, causing unusual wear and tear on the body's circulatory system.

High blood pressure often has no symptoms, so people may not know they suffer from it without being tested. But it is a serious condition, since it can lead to heart disease and strokes.

Although they are far from certain, many experts feel that there is a link between high blood pressure and stress.[4] Stressful events clearly cause temporary increases in blood pressure, and long-term, continuing stress leads to lingering increases. For instance, overcrowding, job stress, and unemployment all increase blood pressure.

Some experts think that high blood pressure is produced when people hide their anger. Others think that people with high blood pressure are unusually sensitive to stress. These people may respond to even trivial stressors with unusually strong physical reactions, paving the way for continual high blood pressure.

EATING DISORDERS: ANOREXIA NERVOSA AND BULIMIA

Stress plays a major part in two disorders that revolve around eating. In *anorexia nervosa,* people refuse to eat because they are afraid of gaining weight and becoming fat. Even though they may actually be skinny, people suffering from anorexia nervosa feel overweight, and so they restrict their intake of food drastically. In 15 to 20 percent of the cases of the disease, the victims end up starving themselves to death.

Anorexia nervosa mainly afflicts young women aged twelve through their early twenties. Those with the disease are often successful, attractive, and from middle- or upper-class families.

A related eating disorder is *bulimia*. In this disease, people eat huge quantities of food during a short period of time. For example, they may eat a whole gallon of ice cream and a package of cookies at a single sitting. However, afterward they feel guilt and depression. Frequently, they then make themselves vomit or take laxatives to remove the food from their body. This cycle is continually repeated, producing chemical imbalances that can lead to death.

It is not known precisely why people develop anorexia nervosa or bulimia. Some scientists think it may be due to a chemical imbalance in the body. However, stress also appears to play an important role in many cases. For example, people with anorexia nervosa frequently say that they feel pressure to do everything well, and those with bulimia are overly concerned about maintaining their popularity.

STRESS AND ILLNESS: A SUMMARY

We have discussed several psychosomatic illnesses that are directly related to stress. It is important to keep in mind, however, that none of the diseases we have discussed is necessarily caused by stress alone. Rather, stress usually is one of several reasons a person develops an illness. And sometimes illnesses occur even when stress is only minimal or not present at all.

Still, it is clear that stress is an important component of several psychosomatic illnesses. We turn now to some of the reasons why stress might produce illness.

HOW DOES STRESS CAUSE ILLNESS?

We saw in Chapter 4 how Selye's General Adaptation Syndrome theory provides an explanation for the negative consequences of stress. But it is a fairly general explanation of the effects of being exposed to a stressor. In particular, it does not cover all the possibilities about how stress might lead to the development of specific illnesses.

Shelley Taylor is a psychologist who specializes in health issues. She has outlined several possibilities about the relationship between stress and illness.[5] They include the following:

1. *Stress directly causes disease due to physical changes in the body.* According to this view, stress directly produces physical declines that eventually lead to disease.

At first, the symptoms caused by stress may be limited to such things as being tired or achy. If people deal immediately with these first symptoms—by getting more sleep, for instance—they may avoid future illness. If they do nothing to reduce the stress, the chance of their coming down with a more severe illness rises as their body's ability to fight off germs declines. In this view, then, it is the experience of stress that leads directly to becoming ill.

2. *Stress produces illness, but only in combination with other physical weakness that already exists.* In this explanation of the route from stress to illness, stress by itself does not produce illness but helps to bring it on in people who are already physically weakened in some way.

For example, elderly people, in general, are more likely to become ill than younger people. Therefore, if an older person is exposed to a strong stressor, he or she is more likely to become ill than a younger person who is affected by the same stressor.

In sum, according to this view, stress by itself is not enough to cause illness. Some other physical weakness, as might be found in the elderly, the poor, or infants, must also be present in order for stress to result in illness.

3. *Stress produces a change in health habits, leading to illness.* In this view, stress leads people to behave in a less healthy way. This unhealthy behavior causes illness.

Suppose, for instance, that your parents begin to fight a lot and you become afraid that they are going to get a divorce. As a reaction to the stress of the situation, you begin to smoke, because you think it may calm you and reduce your stress. By smoking, though, you make it more likely that you will get a variety of lung diseases, including cancer. In sum, by making you act in a less healthy way, stress has made it more probable that you will become sick.

Which of these three explanations of the route between stress and illness is correct?

In fact, all three occur, depending on the strength of the stressor and the particular individual involved. In some people, it is likely that stress by itself is enough to trigger illness. With others, stress will lead to disease only if there is some other weakness already present. In still other people, stress will lead to unhealthy behavior that will end up causing disease.

CHAPTER SIX

STRESS AND MAJOR ILLNESS: HEART DISEASE AND CANCER

Tyrone Pell was starting the day as he usually did. Seated on his exercise bike, he was pedaling away with vigor. He was pleased to be getting his exercise quota for the day.

Tyrone kept careful watch over his speed. He always tried to go faster than he had the day before. He constantly set new goals for himself, and he was never satisfied until he reached them. "I wonder why I can't just do this for the fun of it and not worry about how fast I'm going," he thought to himself.

Actually, it was not only Tyrone's competitiveness that was out of the ordinary. The bike itself was a bit unusual. He had rigged a desktop to the front. This permitted him to read and even jot down notes as he exercised. And because the bike was positioned in front of the television, he was able to watch TV as he pedaled and read.

Tyrone was pleased with himself. How many other people could exercise, read, write, and watch TV—all at the same time?[1]

The truth is, few of us would go to the bother of designing a way to do so many things at once. And this is probably a good thing, because people who hate to waste a moment, like Tyrone, lead lives filled with stress and are more likely than the rest of us to have heart attacks.

It is becoming increasingly clear to scientists that several major diseases once thought to have biological causes are actually related to stress. We will examine how two of the biggest killers, heart disease and cancer, show links to stress.

STRESS AND HEART DISEASE

Tyrone's higher likelihood of a heart attack is the result of a set of traits that are called the *Type-A behavior pattern*.[2] People who have the Type-A behavior pattern are competitive, impatient, and aggressive. They are always rushing, and they create deadlines for themselves—even when they don't need to. Like Tyrone, they try to do several things at once so they won't waste a moment.

People who are Type A's are sometimes hostile to others. Their impatience can make them snap at people, and they can be quite unfriendly to those they think are keeping them from completing a task.

The hostility and competitiveness of the Type A's leads them to experience high levels of stress. They always feel that they are under pressure, and they are always trying to beat the clock. They think that other people work too slowly.

Type A's measure success in terms of how much they produce. Quality is much less important to them; it is quantity that counts.

In contrast to the Type-A behavior pattern is the *Type-B behavior pattern*. People with the Type-B pattern are all the things that Type A's are not.

Type-B people are neither competitive nor aggressive. They show patience in times of stress, not rushing to compete against real or imaginary deadlines. They don't work as hard as Type-A individuals, putting in less hours on the job, and they show little hostility toward others.

TYPE-A BEHAVIOR AND HEART DISEASE

The difference between Type A's and Type B's extends to health. Many surveys have found that people with the Type-A behavior pattern are more likely to develop heart disease. One study looked at 3,000 men who had no signs of heart disease.[3] The study indicated that men who showed the Type-A pattern at the start of the study were twice as likely to develop heart disease after eight years than Type B's. In addition, the Type A's had many more fatal heart attacks than the Type B's.

Clearly, it seems as if there is an association between the Type-A behavior pattern and heart disease. But what, specifically, is the link?

The best answer seems to be that Type A's tend to respond to stressors with more frequent biological reactions than Type B's. Biological reactions include such things as increased heart rate and breathing rates. Furthermore, not only are their biological reactions more frequent, but the intensity of the reaction that occurs is higher in Type A's than Type B's.

In turn, this overreaction to stressors produces frequent emergency reactions. Eventually, this leads to wear and tear on the heart and circulation systems of the body. In the end, it makes Type A's more likely to develop heart disease and have heart attacks than Type B's.

Because the effects of being a Type A begin early, the results build up over a lifetime. For instance, some children show symptoms of Type-A behavior even as early as nursery school. They are competitive, aggressive, and quick to anger. These same children also show more frequent, and stronger, biological reactions to stressors. The Type-A behavior pattern, then, may pave the way for future heart disease beginning at an early age.

If you fit into the Type-A category, does it mean that

you are likely to have a heart attack when you are older? The answer is no for several reasons, and even more emphatically no if you are a female. First, most of what we know about the Type-A behavior pattern applies to men and not necessarily women. Heart disease occurs in men more often than in women. For this reason, scientists have carried out much of their research just with men, and we can't be sure if Type-A behaviors are related to heart disease in women.

Second, we don't know for sure what it is about Type-A behavior that is related to heart disease. For example, some researchers think that it is mostly the high levels of hostility and anger shown by people with the Type-A behavior pattern that is the primary cause of the increase in heart disease. They think that other characteristics of Type-A people may be not as important.

Finally, it is possible that some factor not yet discovered causes both heart disease *and* the Type-A behavior pattern in some people. The research evidence is not at all clear on this question.

Still, it is safe to say that Type A's are more likely to develop heart disease than Type B's. If you are competitive, frequently annoyed with other people, and easily frustrated, you might want to slow down.

STRESS AND CANCER

Most people fear getting cancer more than any other disease. They think of it as causing horrible, lingering pain. They assume that cancer is incurable, and they believe that death is certain.

The facts are different. Many kinds of cancer can be cured, especially if the disease is found early enough. In addition, scientists are learning new facts about the illness every day.

The basic biology of cancer is already well understood. Certain cells in the body become transformed, and they begin to multiply rapidly and uncontrollably. As these cells multiply, they form tumors. The tumors suck nourishment from healthy cells. Eventually, the tumors destroy the body's ability to work normally.

Although scientists are clear on what happens when a person already has cancer, one basic mystery remains: what is the exact trigger of the disease?

There are probably many reasons that cancer begins in a person's body. However, more and more evidence seems to be saying that stress plays some role.

THE CANCER-PRONE PERSONALITY

One of the reasons scientists think that there is a link between stress and cancer is the idea that there may be a *cancer-prone personality*. The cancer-prone personality consists of a set of personality traits that are found more frequently in people who have cancer than those who do not.[4]

What personality traits make up the cancer-prone personality? Most often, people who are polite, unaggressive, and agreeable are said to have this type of personality. They seem to have trouble showing when they are angry. Even in situations in which they should be angry, they appear to be calm and happy.

When faced with a stressful event, people with the cancer-prone personality do not show stress outwardly. Instead, they keep their emotions bottled inside. They repress, or hide, their emotions, even from themselves.

The cancer-prone personality is linked to the likelihood of getting cancer, and the same personality traits seem to help affect a cancer victim's recovery.

For example, some studies have looked at cancer patients who accept the cancer without getting angry.[5] These patients get sick faster and they die sooner than people who become angry at their cancer and fight the disease.

However, it is important to keep in mind that some scientists interpret these research findings differently. First of all, not everyone who has a cancer-prone personality gets cancer. And not everyone who has cancer has a cancer-prone personality.

Even more important, there is no proof that having a cancer-prone personality causes cancer. In fact, it may be the other way around: getting cancer *may cause* people to develop a cancer-prone personality.

STRESSFUL EVENTS AND CANCER

Do stressful events cause people to develop cancer?

Research suggests such a possibility. Cancer patients often report having experienced a high level of stressful life events (the kind we talked about in Chapter 2) before they came down with cancer. In addition, people who undergo high stress are more likely to develop cancer than those who do not.[6]

Studies of animals produce similar results. Rats exposed to stressors are more likely to develop cancer than rats not exposed to the same stressors. The kinds of stressors that produce cancer in animals range from extreme crowding to exposure to uncontrollable electric shock.

One powerful source of stress in humans has to do with a lack of social support. *Social support* is the knowledge that we are part of a group of people who care about us and are interested in us.

The lack of social support is stressful, and it has been related to the development of cancer. The death of a loved one has been linked to cancer. In addition, people who did not have close family ties in childhood are more likely to get cancer than those whose families were close.

In sum, scientists have found clear evidence that cancer is linked to stress. But what is the route by which stress might produce cancer?

One theory is that stress affects the body's immune system. The *immune system* is made up of the parts of the body that resist and fight disease. When a harmful cell or object invades the body, the immune system tries to destroy it. But sometimes the immune system does not work as well as it should. Invading cells resist the immune system attack, and they are able to grow with little interference.

One cause of a poorly functioning immune system is stress. Stress reduces the ability of the immune system to fight off disease.

The immune system, then, provides an explanation for why stress might be related to cancer. Stress reduces the ability of the immune system to fight off invading cells. This weakening of the immune system then permits cancer cells to multiply more easily, which allows the disease to overcome the body's defenses and take over.

It is important to remember that there is no proof that stress is related to cancer. In fact, some scientists feel strongly that the links do not exist at all or are so weak they don't matter. It remains a very controversial question. Until more research is carried out, we won't know for sure how closely stress and cancer are related.

PART III

COPING WITH
AND
PREVENTING
STRESS

CHAPTER SEVEN

COPING WITH STRESS

As president of an electronics business, George Ford led a life filled with stress. He smoked heavily, he drank, and he didn't have much time for exercise. His diet was unhealthy: He wouldn't eat an egg, he says, "unless it was fried in bacon grease."

All this changed, though, when he learned he had heart disease. Now his life is radically different. He exercises and watches his diet carefully. He stopped smoking. And he has slowed down, reducing the stress in his life.

The result: He feels better than ever before, and the progress of his heart disease has been stopped.[1]

Like George Ford, everyone can learn to deal with stress. It may take some effort. It may cause us to change some of our most basic habits. But it can be done.

Our efforts to control, reduce, or learn to live with stress are called *coping*. We all have certain habitual ways of dealing with stress. Most of the time, we don't even know we are coping. Other times, though, we need to make a special effort.

In this chapter, we will consider some of the things that people do to cope with stress. We will first discuss how some of us are better at coping than others. Then we will talk about some of the specific things people do to cope with stress.

COPING STYLE AND STRESS

You may know people who react to the least bit of stress with panic. You may also know individuals who calmly confront stress. They rise to the challenges that stress presents, and they seem relaxed even in the face of the strongest stressors.

A person's method of dealing with stress is what psychologists call *coping style*. Some people naturally cope well with stress, while others have more difficulty.

The people who seem least bothered by stress have a coping style called "hardiness." *Hardiness* is a trait that allows them to deal with stress well.[2] Hardy people have less illness and fewer other negative reactions to stress.

People who show hardiness throw themselves into whatever they do. They have a sense that everything they do is important, at least to them. In addition, these people feel a sense of challenge. They like change and look forward to new situations.

Finally, hardy people feel that they control what happens to them. They feel it is their effort, rather than chance or luck, that influences what takes place.

In sum, people with the trait of hardiness are upbeat, positive people. They try hard to make things happen, and when they face a stressor, they work actively to deal with it.

STRESS AND DEFENSE MECHANISMS

What about the people who don't handle stress well? Some people "protect" themselves from stress by using defense mechanisms. *Defense mechanisms* are ways of hiding stress from oneself and others.[3] Instead of dealing directly with stress, these people avoid thinking about it. They "cope" with stress by pushing the negative feelings into a part of the mind called the "unconscious."

Some psychologists think that in the unconscious part of our minds we have thoughts that we are not aware of. But even though we do not know we have these thoughts, they can affect our behavior.

Many kinds of defense mechanisms are related to stress. Among the most important are those summarized in Table 7-1.

REPRESSION

The defense mechanism that is used most often is repression. In *repression,* thoughts or feelings produced by stress are pushed into the unconscious; we are no longer aware of them.

For example, there are some cases in which adults

Table 7-1
Summary of the Major Defense Mechanisms

Repression—pushing stress-related thoughts or feelings into the unconscious

Suppression—consciously trying to forget unpleasant thoughts

Displacement—shifting negative feelings or thoughts about a powerful, threatening person onto a weaker person

Rationalization—distorting the facts about things that happen in order to justify them

Fantasy—imagining events and achievements

Regression—behaving as one did during an earlier stage of life

---

who were abused as children cannot remember that they were abused. The thought of the abuse is so stressful and painful that the adult completely represses it. But the abuse is not actually forgotten. It just has become part of the unconscious. Eventually, something may trigger the memory, and it can move out of the unconscious and be remembered.

In some ways, repression can be a helpful way of coping with stress. Repression helps us put the problems of the past behind us. That lets us deal with more current sources of stress.

On the other hand, because the memory of the past stressor still lingers in unconscious memory, it can affect our behavior. We may not even be aware of why we are acting the way we do, but we may not be able to cope well with current stress.

SUPPRESSION

Have you ever told yourself to forget about something that was bothering you? If so, you have used suppression. In *suppression,* you voluntarily try to push unpleasant thoughts out of your mind.

Suppression is different from repression. In repression, you are not aware you are forgetting stressful situations. When you suppress something, in contrast, you know you are trying to forget it.

As you might guess, suppression is not a very effective defense mechanism. We all have trouble trying *not* to think about something that is bothering us.

DISPLACEMENT

A teacher has just given you a bad grade on a report. You feel angry, but you know you can't tell the teacher just how furious you really are.

On your way home from school, you catch your younger brother riding your bicycle. Usually this is fine, but today you yell at him, telling him to get off it and to never touch anything that belongs to you again. He gets off the bike and walks away, thinking to himself that your behavior is strange.

Why was your behavior toward your brother so harsh? You displaced your negative feelings and thoughts about a powerful person, your teacher, by shifting them to a weaker person, your little brother.

Displacement may spare a person who is the real object of anger, but it unfairly targets an innocent friend, family member, or even pet. Because of this, displacement can cause misunderstandings and hurt relationships. It is not a very good way of dealing with stress.

RATIONALIZATION

If you are always making excuses for yourself, you may be using the defense mechanism called rationalization. *Rationalization* occurs when people distort the facts to justify bad thoughts, feelings, or events. This allows them to escape the blame and therefore the stress.

For example, students who do poorly on tests sometimes use rationalization to explain their performance. It works this way: Instead of saying that she did not study enough for a test, Barbara claims that the test was unfair. Rationalization makes the poor grade the teacher's fault, not the student's.

Rationalization is sometimes hard to recognize. Often people's arguments seem to make sense. But if you look more carefully, there is often a piece of logic missing.

FANTASY

Before you finish high school, several of the best colleges in the country beg you to enroll. But before you get a chance to enroll, you win six gold medals in the Olympics. Then you are so famous and popular that you are elected president of the United States. After serving two terms, you finally get to go to college.

All of us have fantasies, although most are not as

wild as this one. Fantasies let us develop a sense of control in our lives. They let us build a world that has no risk or pain. They also let us escape from stress, if only for a little while.

If we don't fantasize too much, imagining this "other world" can be a good thing. But too much fantasy is not good. Substituting fantasy for reality can leave us unable to face our problems.

REGRESSION

Have you ever stomped out of a room in anger, slamming the door behind you? If you have, you were exhibiting regression.

Regression is displaying behavior that was characteristic of an earlier stage of life. For instance, stress may cause an alcoholic who has stopped drinking to drink.

Regression is a way people deal with stress by escaping to a previous period of life when they were less mature. This allows them to escape their current problems. Regression, too, is a poor means of dealing with stress.

HOW EFFECTIVE ARE DEFENSE MECHANISMS?

These defense mechanisms and others share a number of characteristics. They are learned reactions to stress. They help us deal with stressors that might otherwise harm us. And we are not aware of them, since they occur in the unconscious part of our minds.

But even though defense mechanisms can help us cope with stress, they are not the best solution. Since they usually involve misinterpreting feelings or events, they keep us from understanding and addressing our problems in a helpful way. In addition, because we are usually not aware that we are using them, we are unable to control them.

In sum, defense mechanisms help protect us from stress, but they can be harmful if they are overused. As we will see, there are more effective ways of dealing with stressors.

CHAPTER EIGHT

CONTROLLING YOUR BIOLOGICAL REACTIONS TO STRESS

The headaches I handle with aspirin, Gelusil for the stomachaches, and a drink for the nerves. It seemed to be working until last Sunday when I noticed my speech slurring and my hand getting numb, then my arm and the right side of my face. I had a stroke.

Imagine me with a stroke. . . . Maybe it's the stress of the job, who knows, but what's new? It's part of my job. . . .

Doctor said I should take it easy. "I'll try, Doc, but can't promise. I mean, to be a cop is to be a stress officer. It's what the job is all about. If I can't cope out there, I might as well be a night watchman in a cemetery."

I guess I've just got to get tougher so the job doesn't get to me the way it does. But *how* to do that is another matter.[1]

To this police officer, coping with stress seems to be an impossible task. It's not.

Hans Selye, the stress expert who devised the GAS

theory, has said, "It is not what happens to you that matters, but how you take it." All of us face stress in our lives, but some of us deal with it better than others.

We turn now to some of the more effective ways of coping with stress. Not all of them will work for everyone. In fact, some may work for you some of the time but not always.

In this chapter we will focus on behavioral changes that affect our physical well-being and help us cope with stress. In the next chapter, we will discuss how modifying our thoughts and emotions can help us deal with stress.

Think back to the body's usual reaction to stress: heartbeat and blood pressure rise, muscles become tense, and we begin to sweat. Our bodies become prepared to either fight or flee the stressor.

Now suppose you could control these natural biological reactions. Could stress's toll on the body be decreased?

Several techniques for coping with stress prove that it can. They are meditation, progressive relaxation, biofeedback, exercise, relaxation and sleep, hypnosis, and diet.

MEDITATION

Om. Doong. Mahn.

Strange sounds like these are often a central part of meditation, a technique that is used to reduce stress. *Meditation* is a procedure for changing what we pay attention to.

In most kinds of meditation, people repeat a sound, word, or syllable such as those listed above. In other kinds, they stare at a picture, a plant, a part of the body, or a flame.

The exact sound or object used is not important. What is important is that people have something to concentrate on. Through concentration, they are no longer aware of anything else.

In effective meditation, several things happen to the body. Heart rate slows. Blood pressure declines. Use of oxygen decreases. The pattern of electrical waves in the brain changes. People say that they feel different, too. After twenty minutes of meditation, they are relaxed and re-freshed. Overall, they feel less stress.

Although no one knows just why meditation works, it does seem to be effective.

PROGRESSIVE RELAXATION

Progressive relaxation is a direct route to relaxing. *Progressive relaxation* is a coping method in which specific muscle groups and the body as a whole are relaxed. People are trained to relax by first tensing and then relaxing parts of the body. This teaches them to recognize and control those muscles.

Progressive relaxation produces several results. After learning to relax specific muscle groups, people report feeling more relaxed in general. The practice also leads to a reduction in high blood pressure and other stress-related diseases. Overall, people say they feel less stress after us-ing this method.

You can try progressive relaxation by using the fol-lowing drill, designed by Herbert Benson, a specialist in stress management:

1. Sit quietly in a comfortable position.

2. Close your eyes.

3. Deeply relax all your muscles. Begin at your feet and move up to your face. Keep them relaxed as you go.

4. Breathe through your nose. Pay attention to your breathing.

5. As you breathe out, say the word "one" silently to yourself. For example, breathe in, out, and say, "one";

then breathe in, out, and say "one"; and keep repeating this.

6. Continue for ten to twenty minutes. You may open your eyes to check the time; do not use an alarm.

7. When you finish, sit quietly for several minutes, at first with your eyes closed and later with your eyes open. Do not stand up for a few minutes.

8. Practice once or twice a day. Do not do it within two hours after any meal.[2]

BIOFEEDBACK

When we first talked about the effects of stress on the body, we discussed how heart rate, blood pressure, and breathing occur automatically and continually, without any thought on our part.

Until a few years ago, most scientists thought we had no control over such operations of the body. However, new research has found just the opposite.[3]

Biofeedback teaches us to control internal biological processes. Connecting a person to an electronic device provides information about specific biological processes. With this information, the individual is able to learn to control those processes.

For example, suppose a woman wanted to stop headaches produced by muscle tension in her neck. She would connect electronic sensors to her neck, which would show when the muscles were tight and when they were loose. Then, she would see what she could do to relax the muscles. And after enough practice, she would learn how to increase her muscle relaxation, even when she was not hooked up to the electronic equipment.

Biofeedback has been shown to be effective in teaching people to reduce a variety of biological responses, including headaches and pain. Even though it isn't always successful and it requires work with an expert, it shows promise for controlling stress.

EXERCISE

Meditation, progressive relaxation, and biofeedback share a common principle: the best way to cope with stress is to reduce the body's biological reactions to stressors. But there is another technique that reduces stress, one that is based on very different reasoning. The idea is to increase the body's biological reactions—at least for a short time—through exercise.

Exercise is a surprisingly effective way of dealing with stress. First of all, many of the biological signs of stress are relieved by exercise. People who exercise regularly have slower heartbeats, reduced rates of breathing, and lower blood pressure when they are resting.

Exercise does something else. Besides keeping their minds off their problems for the time being, it gives people a sense of control over their bodies. They can feel its effects very concretely.

When people exercise vigorously, chemicals called "endorphins" are generated in the brain. Endorphins are natural painkillers. They can even make us feel happy. For instance, you may know people who say that they get a "runner's high" when they jog. A "runner's high" is an uplifting feeling that results from a long run. Most scientists think that a "runner's high" is caused by the release of endorphins.[4]

In sum, exercise is a good way to cope with stress. It relieves biological symptoms of stress, makes us feel better, and is good for our general health.

RELAXATION AND SLEEP

It is not uncommon for people under stress to have trouble sleeping. They may wake in the night and have trouble getting back to sleep, or they may be unable to get to sleep in the first place.

It follows that one effective way of coping with stress would be to relax more and get more sleep. Simply taking

time out during the day to sit back and unwind helps us deal with stress.

Even more important is finding ways to get a good night's sleep. Sticking to a regular bedtime is important, because it allows the body to depend on a regular schedule.

Drinks that contain caffeine, a chemical that keeps people awake, should be avoided. Coffee, tea, and many soft drinks have large amounts of caffeine. People who have trouble sleeping should not drink anything with caffeine in it within six hours of going to bed. In contrast, drinking a glass of warm milk often helps people sleep better.

In sum, relaxation and sleep can be improved, and both can help us cope with stress.

HYPNOSIS

You've probably seen hypnosis done by entertainers. Members of the audience are put into a trance and made to carry out all sorts of silly behaviors. *Hypnosis*, though, can be used for more than entertainment. People under hypnosis are easily influenced. The hypnotist can make suggestions to be followed even after an individual is no longer under hypnosis.[5]

People who are hypnotized can be told to control their biological reactions to stressors. For example, they may be directed to breathe more slowly and deeply when exposed to a stressor.

Unfortunately, hypnosis is not foolproof. Some people cannot be hypnotized at all. Others do not follow the

These girls row crew together. Physical exercise can help reduce stress, and the camaraderie of team effort is an added uplift.

hypnotist's orders well. But when it is successful, it can help people cope better with stress.

DIET

A change in diet is sometimes effective in dealing with stress. Some experts feel that stress is related to the level of sugar in the blood. By eating more carefully, we can regulate sugar and experience less stress.

There are other ways that diet is related to stress. Some of us react to stress by devouring our favorite foods. This can put a strain on our bodies, which may lead to even greater stress.

Similarly, being overweight can act as a stressor. Eating a more healthy diet and keeping fit are two of the best ways to reduce stress.

In this chapter, we have focused on biological ways to change the body's reactions to stress. However, this is just one aspect of coping with stress. It is just as important to cope with stress psychologically. The next chapter deals with the psychological means of coping.

CHAPTER NINE

MANAGING AND PREVENTING STRESS

"I failed the test. This just proves I really am stupid. I'll never do any better in school. I'm just a flop. I just can't deal with the stress of school."

—Henry Opot

"I failed the test. I've got to plan better next time. I'll work out a study schedule. I'll meet with the teacher after school. I know I can deal better with the stress of school."
—Luellen Fiske

As you can see from the two comments above, the same situation can produce very different responses.

Henry Opot is giving up. He sees the situation as hopeless and out of his control. His statements are not logical. Doing badly on a test doesn't prove he is stupid, and it does not mean that he can't do any better in the future.

Luellen Fiske is able to cope with the stress of her failure. She plans for the future and tells herself that she can improve. Hers is a logical approach.

Rather than dealing with their stress from a biological standpoint, Henry and Luellen are using a psychological approach.

In this chapter, we will see that changing our thoughts, emotions, and feelings about a situation can be an effective way to deal with stress.

REDEFINING THE MEANING OF STRESSORS: REAPPRAISAL

Do you remember the definition of "stress" given in the beginning of this book? We said that stress occurs when situations are appraised, or thought of, as threatening or challenging. If we see a circumstance as a threat or a challenge, it will produce stress. But we can reappraise a situation by looking for its positive aspects. A threatening situation can become a problem we can solve.

Of course, this will not reduce stress entirely. Even challenging, positive circumstances produce stress. But positive stressors are normally less stressful than negative ones.

Suppose you learned that your family was going to move and that you would have to change schools. You would probably appraise the situation as entirely negative—and it would be quite stressful. Now consider the positive aspects of the change: moving into a new house, perhaps having your own room for the first time, and making new friends, for example. When you appraise the situation in this way, moving may become more of an adventure than a threat, and you will feel less stress. All it takes is a new attitude about the situation.

REACTING TO STRESSORS: STRESS INOCULATION

If you, like Henry Opot, ever felt frustrated enough to give up trying, you are not alone. Most of us feel this way from time to time. In fact, many of us have thoughts that are not only quite illogical but harmful to our efforts to cope

A student studying for a test. If you confront
such sources of stress as an upcoming test by
doing the necessary preparations (i.e., studying),
your overall level of anxiety will
be considerably lessened.

with stress. Some people expect love and approval all the time. Some feel they must always be successful, never failing at anything. And many people think that it is terrible when things don't always go the way they want them to.

Clearly, such beliefs are not realistic. No one's life is perfect, and to expect perfection only leads to frustration and stress.

Psychologist Donald Meichenbaum says that recognizing that we hold these illogical expectations may help us to better cope with stress. He has developed *stress-inoculation training,* a three-part procedure for teaching people to rethink the stressors in their lives.[1] The procedure calls for:

1. *Learning to be more aware of our thoughts and actions.* To do this, we keep a daily diary, which helps us to recognize the specific situations that produce stress for us. Once we recognize our stressors, we can address and gain control over them.

2. *Beginning to practice logical thoughts and behaviors.* For example, we may say to ourselves, "This isn't as bad as it seems. I'm going to be OK." With this approach, we get into the habit of facing stress in a more constructive way. (See Table 9-1.)

3. *Putting the skills we have learned into practice.* This means that we deal with increasingly stressful situations until using the statements in Table 9-1 becomes a habit. We then are taught to reward ourselves by telling ourselves what a good job we did.

Stress inoculation has been shown to be effective, but it does not always work. Sometimes people cannot escape from stress no matter what they tell themselves.

But the frequent success of the method shows how important it is to be prepared; knowing how to cope with stress is half the battle.

Table 9-1
Stress-Inoculation Training Statements *

To better confront stressful situations, people are taught these statements during stress-inoculation training:

Preparation statements:
  What do I have to do?
  I can develop a plan to deal with it.
  Maybe what I think of as anxiety is eagerness to confront the stressor.
  Don't worry; worry won't help anything.

Confrontation statements:
  Take things one step at a time; I can handle the situation.
  This anxiety is what I thought would happen and have been told I would feel. It's a reminder to use my coping exercises.
  Relax; I'm in control.
  Take a slow, deep breath.

Coping statements:
  When fear comes, just pause a minute.
  Keep the focus on the present; what is it I have to do?
  I can't eliminate fear totally; just keep it manageable.

Self-reward statements:
  It worked; I did it.
  Wait until I tell someone about this.
  It wasn't as bad as I expected.
  It's getting better each time I use the method.

* Adapted from D. Meichenbaum, *Cognitive Behavior Modification: An Integration* (New York: Plenum Publishing Corporation, 1977). Reprinted by permission of Plenum Publishing Corporation.

TURNING TO OTHERS: SEEKING SOCIAL SUPPORT

One of the best ways of dealing with stress is to turn to others. Their social support helps us cope in a number of ways.[2] Knowing that we are valued provides emotional support. Information from friends can help us study more effectively, resolve conflicts in our relationships, cope with a difficult teacher, and find time for a part-time job.

Finally, having a support network can provide material help. For survivors of natural disasters, social support comes in the form of gifts of food and clothing and the rebuilding of homes that have burned down.

In sum, social support helps reduce stress, and it helps us cope with stress more effectively.

ESCAPING THE STRESSOR

Being a "quitter" is something most people try to avoid. We are taught that sticking things out, no matter how hard they get, is mature behavior.

Sometimes though, the truth is, leaving a stress-producing situation is a more reasonable approach; choosing "flight" over "fight" can sometimes be the best solution.[3]

Let's consider this situation: You have an after-school job helping an elderly neighbor with small chores around his house. For the first month the job is a pleasure, and it doesn't conflict with your home life or your schoolwork. Then, one day, your parents tell you they need you to care for your younger sister three afternoons a week. This means working longer hours and spending every evening on your homework.

First you face the stressor. You explain to your neighbor that you'll have to cut back your time with him. You work extra hard during free periods at school. But before you know it, your grades start slipping and you have no time to relax.

You confronted the stressor, but things got worse. It's time to flee: you give up your after-school job, and your life returns to normal.

How do you know when it is time to flee from a stressful situation? First, make a serious effort to confront the stress. If you are unsuccessful, it may be time to put the situation behind you.

Second, look at the alternatives to staying in the situation. If you find that other choices seem better, then it may be wise to leave. On the other hand, you may find that all the possible alternatives are just as bad as the current situation. In that case, it may not make sense to make a change.

Finally, you should try to reduce stress in other areas of your life. If your stress is still so high that you can't function well, then it may be time to leave the situation.

Of course, people cannot flee from every situation. But when it is possible, removing oneself from a stressful situation might make the most sense.

IS STRESS ALWAYS BAD?

Consider for a moment what it would be like if we were free from all stress and were never challenged or threatened. Life would be routine, boring, and maybe even dreary. If we never faced any challenges, we would never feel the satisfaction of overcoming difficulties. In a sense, then, stress helps us grow.

Stress also leads people to a better awareness of the world by making them consider the hurdles they confront. In times of real crisis, stress can give us the will, the strength, and the energy to fight back.

Stress also helps us evaluate our goals. It can make us hold more realistic objectives. And it can keep us from making the same mistakes twice.

Finally, stress may help us feel more capable. If we

confront stress and win, we will feel better about ourselves. Facing and overcoming stress is a very positive experience.

Although stress provides one of life's major challenges, it is necessary. It can help us grow and become better people. In the end it can help us reach our full potential.

SOURCE NOTES

Chapter 1

1. D. Robinson, "Stressbusters," *Parade,* July 22, 1990, 12–13.
2. S. Breznitz and L. Goldberger, "Stress Research at a Crossroads," in L. Goldberger and S. Breznitz, eds., *Handbook of Stress: Theoretical and Clinical Aspects* (New York: Free Press, 1982).
3. K. A. Holroyd and R. S. Lazarus, "Stress, Coping, and Somatic Adaptation," in Goldberger and Breznitz.
4. S. Taylor, *Health Psychology* (Reading, Mass.: Addison-Wesley, 1986).

Chapter 2

1. R. S. Lazarus and J. B Cohen, "Environmental Stress," in I. Altman and J. F. Wohlwill, eds., *Human Behavior and the Environment: Current Theory and Research,* vol. 2 (New York: Plenum, 1977).
2. T. H. Holmes and R. H. Rahe, "The Social Adjustment Rating Scale," *Journal of Psychosomatic Research,* 11 (1967), 213–218.
3. D. V. Perkins, "The Assessment of Stress Using Life Events Units Scales, in L. Goldberger and S. Breznitz, eds., *Handbook of Stress: Theoretical and Clinical Aspects* (New York: Free Press, 1982).
4. B. S. Dohrenwend, B. P. Dohrenwend, M. Dodson, and P. E. Shrout, "Symptoms, Hassles, Social Supports, and Life Events: The Problem of Confounded Measures," *Journal of Abnormal Psychology* 93 (1984), 1222–230; and B. Lakey, K. Heller, "Response Biases and the Relation between Negative Life Events and Psychological Symptoms," *Journal of Personality and Social Psychology* 49 (1985), 1662–1668.
5. N. Bolger, A. DeLongis, R. C. Kessler, and E. A. Schilling, "Effects of Daily Stress on Negative Mood," *Journal of Personality and Social Psychology* 57 (1989), 808–818.

Chapter 3

1. A. Baum, "Disasters, Natural and Otherwise," *Psychology Today*, April 1988, 57–60.
2. A. Baum, R. Fleming, and J. E. Singer, "Coping with Technological Disaster," *Journal of Social Issues* 39 (1983), 117–138.
3. M. Horowitz, *Stress Response Syndrome*, 2d ed. (New York: Jason Aronson, 1986).
4. A. Baum, R. J. Gatchel, and M. A. Schaeffer, "Emotional, Behavioral, and Physiological Effects of Chronic Stress at Three Mile Island," *Journal of Consulting and Clinical Psychology* 51 (1983), 565–572.
5. G. Bennet, "Bristol Floods, 1968: Controlled Survey of Effects on Health of Local Community Disaster," *British Medical Journal* 3 (1970), 454–458.
6. R. C. Carson, J. N. Butcher, and J. C. Coleman, *Abnormal Psychology and Modern Life*, 8th ed. (Glenview, Ill.: Scott, Foresman, 1988).
7. L. Roberts, "Vietnam's Psychological Toll," *Science* 243 (July 7, 1988), 481–482.

Chapter 4

1. W. B. Cannon, *Bodily Changes in Pain, Hunger, Fear, and Rage*, 2d ed. (Boston: Charles T. Branford, 1953).
2. H. Selye, *The Stress of Life* (New York: McGraw-Hill, 1978).
3. J. W. Mason, "Specificity in the Organization of Neuroendocrine Response Profiles," in P. Seeman and G. M. Brown, eds., *Frontiers in Neurology and Neuroscience Research: First International Symposium of the Neuroscience Institute* (Toronto: University of Toronto Press, 1974); and A. Mikhail, "Stress: A Psychophysiological Conception," *Journal of Human Stress* 7 (1981), 9–15.

Chapter 5

1. Based on a case history cited in N. Cameron, *Personality Development and Psychology: A Dynamic Approach* (Boston: Houghton Mifflin, 1963), p. 306.
2. T. F. Mucha and R. F. Reinhardt, "Conversion Reactions in Student Aviators," *American Journal of Psychiatry* 127 (1970), 493–497.

3. J. D. Sargent, "Stress and Headaches," in L. Goldberger and S. Breznitz, eds., *Handbook of Stress: Theoretical and Clinical Aspects* (New York: Freeman, 1982).
4. J. E. Byassee, "Essential Hypertension," in R. B. Williams, Jr., and W. D. Gentry, eds., *Behavioral Approaches to Medical Treatment* (Cambridge, Mass.: Ballinger, 1977).
5. S. E. Taylor, *Health Psychology* (Reading, Mass.: Addison-Wesley, 1986).

Chapter 6
1. Based on a case reported in R. S. Feldman, *Adjustment: Applying Psychology in a Complex World* (New York: Mc-Graw-Hill, 1989).
2. P. D. Evans, "Type A Behaviour and Coronary Heart Disease: When Will the Jury Return?" *British Journal of Psychology* 81 (1990), 147–157.
3. R. H. Rosenman, R. J. Brand, C. D. Jenkins, M. Friedman, R. Straus, and M. Wurm, "Coronary Heart Disease in the Western Collaborative Group Study: Final Follow-up Experience of 8½ Years," *Journal of the American Medical Association* 233 (1975), 872–877.
4. E. Smith, "Fighting Cancerous Feelings," *Psychology Today,* May, 1988, 22–23.
5. K. W. Pettingale, T. Morris, S. Greer, and J. L. Haybittle, "Mental Attitudes to Cancer: An Additional Prognostic Factor," *Lancet* (1985), 750.
6. T. H. Holmes, and M. Masuda, "Life Change and Illness Susceptibility," in B. S. Dohrenwend and B. P. Dohrenwend, eds., *Stressful Life Events: Their Nature and Effects* (New York: Wiley, 1974).

Chapter 7
1. *Time,* March 26, 1984, 56.
2. K. D. Allred, and T. W. Smith, "The Hardy Personality: Cognitive and Physiological Responses to Evaluative Threat," *Journal of Personality and Social Psychology* 56 (1989), 257–266.
3. R. C. Carson, J. N. Butcher, and J. C. Coleman, *Abnormal Psychology and Modern Life,* 8th ed. (Glenview, Ill.: Scott, Foresman, 1988).

Chapter 8

1. C. Maslach, *Burnout—The Cost of Caring* (Englewood Cliffs, N.J.: Prentice-Hall, 1982), p. xii.
2. H. Benson, *The Relaxation Response* (New York: Morrow, 1975).
3. N. E. Miller, "Rx: Biofeedback," *Psychology Today* (February 1985), 54–59.
4. B. Hathaway, "Running to Ruin," *Psychology Today* (July 1984), 14–15.
5. E. R. Hilgard (1975). "Hypnosis," *Annual Review of Psychology* 26, 1–26.

Chapter 9

1. D. Meichenbaum, and M. E. Jaremko, eds., *Stress Reduction and Prevention* (New York: Plenum, 1983).
2. G. A. Dakof, and S. E. Taylor, "Victims' Perceptions of Social Support: What Is Helpful from Whom?" *Journal of Personality and Social Psychology* 58 (1990), 80–89.
3. S. Roth, and L. J. Cohen, "Approach, Avoidance, and Coping with Stress," *American Psychologist* 41 (1986), 813–819.

HOW TO FIND OUT MORE ABOUT STRESS

Organizations

American Institute of Stress, 124 Park Avenue, Yonkers, NY 10703

Center for Mental Health Studies of Emergencies, National Institute of Mental Health, 5600 Fishers Lane, Rockville, Md 20857

Books

Benson, H. *The Relaxation Response*. New York: Morrow, 1975.

Borysenko, J. *Minding the Body, Mending the Mind*. Reading, MA: Addison-Wesley, 1987.

Brallier, L. *Successfully Managing Stress*. Los Altos, CA: National Nursing Review, 1982.

Brown, B. *Between Health and Illness*. Boston: Houghton Mifflin, 1984.

Burchfield, S. R., ed. *Stress: Psychological and Physiological Interactions*. Washington, DC: Hemisphere, 1985.

Garmezy, N. "Stressors of Childhood." In N. Garmezy and M. Rutter, eds., *Stress, Coping, and Development in Children*. New York: McGraw-Hill, 1984.

Humphrey, J. H. *Profiles in Stress*. New York: AMS Press, 1986.

———. *Stress in Childhood*. New York: AMS Press, 1984.

Lystad, M., Innovations in Mental Health Services to Disaster Victims. Washington, D.C.: National Institute of Mental Health, 1985.

Selye, H. *Stress without Distress*. Philadelphia: Lippincott, 1974.

Taylor, S. E. *Health Psychology*. New York: McGraw-Hill, 1991.

INDEX

ABOUT THE AUTHOR

Robert S. Feldman is professor of psychology at the University of Massachusetts at Amherst. He has published numerous scientific articles and a best-selling textbook, *Understanding Psychology*. Dr. Feldman holds degrees from Wesleyan University and the University of Wisconsin at Madison. He lives in Amherst with his wife and three children.